No Stranger Than My Own

CONUNDRUM PRESS
A Division of Samizdat Publishing Group, LLC.

ISBN: 978-0-9713678-8-3

Library of Congress Cataloging-in-Publication Data is available upon request.

Conundrum Press books may be purchased with bulk discounts for educational, business, or sales promotional use. For information please email: info@conundrum-press.com

Conundrum Press online: conundrum-press.com

No Stranger Than My Own

Poems

MICHAEL J. HENRY

Acknowledgments

I'd like to thank the following journals for publishing the following poems: *Buffalo Bones*: "A Fever of Pollen"; *Beacon Street Review*: "A Tree For You"; *Open Windows 2007*: "Giacometti"; *Painted Moon Review*: "Deidre Plays Bass For Me," *Pleiades*: "When It Disobeys"; *Poetry Daily*: "Light"; *Red Rock Review*: "The Far Badlands"; *Threepenny Review*: "Albany Winter," *Poetry Motel*: "Edward Hopper's Travels," and *Wazee*: "Horses."

There are so many people who've helped me on the journey to this book, and I truly appreciate their inspiration and guidance. I'd especially like to thank my teachers, Jarold Ramsey, James Longenbach, Bill Knott, John Skoyles, and Gail Mazur. I'd also like to thank my friends and fellow writers, William Haywood Henderson, Jennifer Vacchiano, Lisa Sporte, and all the writers and teachers at Lighthouse Writers Workshop. I'd also like to thank the Colorado Council on the Arts and Platte-Forum, whose fellowships aided greatly in the writing of this book. And special thanks to Chris Ransick for his generous spirit and wisdom in helping me put this book together. Most of all, I'd like to thank my wife, Andrea Dupree, for her endless patience and general smarts, and my daughters, for turning every day into a miracle.

For Em and Jo
and
Andrea

CONTENTS

PART ONE

Edward Hopper's Travels	13
Tomatoes	15
Blood	16
Cadillac, An Ode	18
Giacometti	19
Singing Beach	21
Men In Vegas	22
Pocket Watch	24
Lemonade	26
Solo Renga	27
Loud Music, Neighbor	29
Dreaming Of John Ashbery	31
The Apple	33

PART TWO

A Tree For You	37
Home, The Last Time	39
Contact	41
The Truth About Poetry	43
Broke Down	44
Pack Mentality	46
A Fever Of Pollen	48
When It Disobeys	49
Complications	50
Horses	51
A Bargain For Joe	53
Deidre Plays Bass For Me	54
Elvis Ideal	55

PART THREE

Thruway Mall Atrium, 1980	61
On Safari	63
Light	65
Halloween Satellite	66
At The Water	67
Dolphinettes	68
Ned Falls	70
Albany Winter	71
October Travels, Wind River Range	72
Whisper, In A Dark Suit	73
The Far Badlands	74
Ode To The Pacifiers	76
Blue Haze, Goodnight Moon	78

PART ONE

. . . I'm on the lookout
For the bone, the skeleton half buried
In the leaves, the body sprinkled hastily
With dirt and sticks, the open hand, the plain
Disheveled face no stranger than my own.

—James Longenbach, *"What You Find in the Woods"*

EDWARD HOPPER'S TRAVELS

Edward Hopper's shoes have worn through again
so he writes a note to himself: *need cardboard feet.*
As the trolley rocks under Boylston Street
he feels like a naïve child,
wonders why there's suffering in the world,
why god leaves us to
worry about dust in corners, worn soles, polio.
What is it that's so intriguing and depleting about a
stained bed sheet? He welcomes the stops
at each station, they punctuate his interior
monologue; he's tired of his mind,
tired of *chiaroscuro*, the appalling
emptiness of American sky lit by hard sun.
Eating *veal parmigana* from a crumpling
foil pan, he's glad it's still warm
after hours wandering streets.
Around him, wing-tips, broad silk ties,
flared nostrils wishing for his
dinner. He doesn't care if they stare,
if he dribbles red sauce on his shirt,
already smeared with vermilion oilpaint,
color risen from brush and rag.
He is something to view—
the lonely genius artist—hair unkempt,
eyes a half-drawn window shade,
invitation to look in and barrier all the same.
He thinks a line from Eliot, a key clicks its groove
against tumblers of a lock, the deadbolt
of human kindness. The extinction of personality,
hard like the front steps of a brownstone tenement,
a place to rest his aching legs as the city
rolls away. A silence which redeems,

like a storefront at seven a.m.,
like an empty doorway in September noon.
Like the barren trolley stop Edward Hopper
walks through, his shoes wearing down and down.

TOMATOES

After Stephen Dobyns

I'm on a parapet looking down
at upturned faces and voices
rising like feathers in an
updraft. I am afraid of heights but know
I will fall, and in the knowing my fear
is singed, my will is a skeleton bound
by silver twine, on my cold wrists
there are bracelets, inlaid turquoise with silver
hammered thin by a Hopi in Arizona,
a boy whose face is wide and soft, who blinks
each time the small hammer strikes.
I once had a girl, once lived in the gray
cosmos of her cigarette smoke, her
dark-paneled room, her gold-brown eyes
and face so finely wrought,
like porcelain. The way she brushed
her hair down across
her scapula and vertebrae left me
weak, I thought I might turn
to a feather and drift away.
She had a friend whose name was Paige
who had a mother who did away
with herself on the summer solstice,
four bottles of pills while sitting
in a chaise lounge by a thicket of
tomato vines overgrown and unkempt,
the red planets so full and heavy,
and Paige said every day
that August she ate them
with a pinch of salt,
she said they tasted
like nothing, nothing at all,
like air, she said.

BLOOD

Small ruby, precious stone,
issuing forth from the smallest
hole I've made in my thumb,

bright swarming
along grooves
of fingerprint, swirls and circles

of selfhood, glistening
mushroom cap, billowing
out, enticing me to

bring you to my mouth,
taste my own juice,
the marrow-made code

of helix, ladder of letters:
A-T, C-G. Platelets, ferrous oxide,
chain link to oh-two,

donut-disks floating
alveoli to artery to auricle,
through never-worn flap

into ventricle. Dark tomb,
sack of collection,
spark across synapse,

clasp down small
like a spooked armadillo,
pocket full of disks thrown out

through channels, two roads
diverging in the forest of flesh
to dispense in-breath, anti-speech,

and now you come, outside.
Vermilion, sanguine, crimson,
royal velvet. Pin-prick thick

globe, I take you into my mouth and you
taste like a copper penny. You are
warm and my thumb is clean, the outer

shell of collagen and dermis sealed,
sticky plates closing your blossom down,
keeping in the pretty little secrets.

CADILLAC, AN ODE

Sphinx-like it rests in the driveway, a cherry-red convertible,
red leather seats, white canvas top, shining chrome line down
the center of the hood, the insignia a family shield
with fern leaves curled, the hub caps a hundred gleaming
spokes, fat white-walls, the engine a furnace-block hunk of steel,
a 28-gallon gas tank tucked under a trunk which could fit three
dead guys, a hyperbole of luggage, a cooler packed with
Northern Pike, or my grandfather's shotguns in custom leather
cases. A 1968 Coupe d'Ville, gift from the International Brotherhood
of Teamsters, Local 449, we get in and he drives into the bright
Buffalo sunset, and beyond the breakwall Lake Erie shudders
blue-gray as he reaches down for the CB radio,
which looks like a phone, as the engine tracks the press
of his foot, urges the long red boat headlong, thrumming and
floating on the road, my grandfather's meaty left hand—
middle finger cut off at the last knuckle, a smooth stub—
light on the steering wheel, ring of red, so delicate and thin.

GIACOMETTI

Once, she sent me a postcard of Giacometti
walking past one of his statues—
body tilted forward, hair out of place,
sinewy limbs like the bronze figure beside him.
Art mirrors life, she says, and sometimes

it gets warped. She has soft gold hair
on the back of her sloping gentle neck, she says
she comes every time we make love,
a sharp tug on a string
up and tingling her back.

I never believed her, but then I read
a feature in *Esquire* that supported
what she said, so now I believe her.
We play a game where I say simple things
and she answers with a word:

locker, shower, fingers.
Her reply: *photograph, secrets, lemons.*
Walking through the med center near school
we got lost once, went down
the wrong hallway, came upon

a solitary waiting gurney.
She loved the gentle folds
of the blue velvet bodybag,
the yellow script on the side,
Monroe County Coroner's Office

stitched just below the zipper. The body
inside must have been thin and not too tall;
I did and did not want to touch it, just to
feel the velvet. She wanted to pry open the zipper
and see the face, feel the cold skin of death.

I whispered, *sky, cloth, wheel, nails.* She answered,
touch, stitch, slashed, file. We began walking,
hunched forward as we left the velvet body.
She said the face would've been made of bronze,
gold and shimmering like a priceless statue.

SINGING BEACH

Manchester-by-the-sea, Massachusetts

Wind pushes sand and my skin burns.
The shore is closing down, winter-weary;
green waves rise to crumple white and crazy.

I've not forgotten you. Each day you rise
up and bloom when I am lost in other things.
The image is always rasped clean,

backed by dunes and haze;
your thick hair, short and gray,
your voice in a thousand tones

speaking a million words,
crimson lips and palate,
glistening chords in your unreal

throat. What you say I cannot hear, I am
dead to it, but what if you found me here,
blue-lipped, in the spindrift of

last light, what would you say of my
crooked shoulders, darkening eyes—
your eyes, when you had a body?

Or is your voice the wind on the waves,
and what song are you singing,
and what do you want me to say?

MEN IN VEGAS

At the Sands a gambler's hands
shake, open, then wilt when he throws
the dice. Somewhere near,

behind velvet-padded doors,
there is a vast stage. Spotlight: three ziggurats.
On each, a lazy white tiger.

*

In the 2nd Honeymoon suite, a vacationing
Teamster steps on a bathroom scale.
The numbers whisk past 299,

stop at 12. He is proud,
looking at the dial
between stubby, sausage toes.

*

Around the bus station
where people sleep on newspaper
a man encumbers

his skin with dirt and dust, layered
history. He admires his tanned forearms,
sunless and earthy.

*

Miles away a black-haired man
digs post-holes in stubborn ground.
In his head he hears what

his father once said—
you're too much a girl to be mine.
His childhood: on the gray froth

of Lake Erie, smoke jutting
from steel plant black stacks
where men fire ore into lava,

he fishes, a red-and-white bobber.
His father, hunched by the prow,
stares blank at the waves.

*

In a faceless townhome condo
a man in goatee wakes. He brews
a bunch of coffee, sits on a

miniscule porch in a faded crimson robe.
A pen and notebook wait for words.
He writes nothing.

Every second, the heat crawls farther down
his throat. He exhales,
each breath a small misery.

POCKET WATCH

Keeper of secrets in the dark places
of each night,

you are smooth like an orange or sack
full of coins,

stone yo-yo, sixty-two degrees in my palm.
Once lost

in a closet, the smell of Brylcreem and horse-hair,
snug in an old vest

pocket, tickless, a riverstone.
When I taste you

there is apple, woodsmoke, frozen
broccoli,

chocolate chips. When I wind you
you tap

with greased efficiency like someone's
grandfather clock

but you are a hypnotist's pendulum, a necklace
for a waist,

a trinket of steadfastness, stogies and
bowties,

locator of moment, dragging me along
when all I want

is to *go back*, to when things were safe,
when I was

waist-high and there was sunshine each day
and nothing

to want for, nothing to fuss over.
You make me

course ahead like a shark, which is a
good thing.

When you are in my palm I am
happy and rich,

my tongue clicks, my heart says *One*
every second.

LEMONADE

In the small kitchen
on the white table
lies a single
lemon. I am riding
a bicycle
on the stairs

coming down,
bumpity bump,
but the cycle
grows small
and then
it's a pretzel

between my knees.
Nothing is ever easy.
I am thirsty.
I go to the lemon
and screw it open.
It has

a plastic cap.
I drink
and drink.
Cold, sweet, and tart.
I will never quench
this thirst.

SOLO RENGA

A fat tree cutter
grinds through a thick trunk, teeth clenched—
he's pissed at his boss.

Accounts Payable must have
a Purchase Order reference.

The thesaurus says
that *drunk* is a synonym
for *pixilated.*

Jesus is a metaphor
for the spirit within you.

Father Naumann said
"Fuck You, Jesuits," in class
once, before our prayer.

Monkeys teach their young to eat
ants with long, thin, bamboo sticks.

Like a bull in a
china store, please be careful
parking the Lexus.

A back-seat boom-box plays rap
music from the fuchsia car.

Sonny and Cher sing
"Love Me" on their comedy
show; they're a duet.

Clint Eastwood's slogan for mayor
was, "Go ahead... make me mayor."

Out west, the sunrise
burns through the old wood of a
ghost town left to waste.

Burnt orange over the Charles—
the lights from Fenway come on.

LOUD MUSIC, NEIGHBOR

He cannot take the loud uproar,
it's in every room. It rolls
like the swirls of his ears,
it creases his brow
like cheap vinyl siding.
The door of his mouth opens
and the hinges of jaw creak
then close. Wooden lips
are cracked and dry
and the thin gap
of mouth is leaking
light across the floor of
his speechless mouth.
The Beastie Boys' "No Sleep Till Brooklyn"
thunks and vibrates
the ceiling of his skull
and presses down all thoughts
between the lumpy mattress
and box spring, ferreting away
the lyrics between
two soft fabric slabs
near a stain of indeterminate
origin, like a wad of cash.
His unblinking eyes
are windows but not
windows to his soul,
they are single-paned and old,
they hang on wasted rope,
the glass settled, streaked
and warped by age.
But when he thinks of you,
the music fades,
it does not beat
or crack the plaster walls

of his head, though you are
there, inside the room of his mind.
You see what he sees
through those glazed windows,
standing by the bed
watching dust motes drift
in sun-sparkling air.
You belong to him now
and may not leave until
he forgets your face,
the one he keeps
in a gold picture frame
on the wall.

DREAMING OF JOHN ASHBERY

And only in the light of lost words
Can we imagine our rewards. —John Ashbery

When the phone rings I know who it is,
there are no other possibilities.
John Ashbery's on the line, telling me
I've been elected to the American

Academy of Poets. He's going to
FedEx airline tickets, first class
to Washington, for the ceremony.
He tells me to bring a suit and

swim-flippers, we're going snorkeling
in the Potomac with Bob Lowell
and Bob Pinsky and Bobby Frost.
I'm going to get a medal hung

round my neck, just like his, which he calls
"tacky but munificent." Mr. Ashbery
reminds me to bring business cards, because
connections are important—"It's not what

you know it's who you know," he offers,
sighing over the cliché.
Behind his voice, I hear a piano
playing off and on. A woman's voice mingles

with a child's. I did not know John Ashbery
had children but this is a dream and I scratch
my forearm and stare at my bare feet.
Somehow I know he has a grandchild

at his brownstone in Manhattan.
He cups his hand over
the mouthpiece but I still hear him:
"Way to go honey," he says to the girl

playing scales, and then I see John Ashbery
in a gallery somewhere,
viewing a Kandinsky, a Motherwell, a Clyfford Still, a Rothko,

an eyeglasses arm in his mouth,
and then I see him walking across
a fallow field in Rochester.
He's wearing white safari shorts,

his legs long, white, and hairless.
Knobby knees. At the edge of the field
he comes upon an abandoned
tractor, burgundy and rust.

There he is, in the green buzzing field
and I'm a camera, not a person dreaming.
The award is gone, the phone call
is gone, we are outdoors, and I

cease to exist. I am an eye
unblinking, an ear that hears
the girl playing scales
amidst singing insects, notes tripping

lightly as John Ashbery
stares at the tractor, hands in pockets,
his mind working over a scene
lit by the light of lost words.

THE APPLE

My hand is out in front of me, a large red apple balanced on my palm. I am with my dad. He's twenty yards away, loading his rifle, and I'm not nervous, he's a good shot, has perfect vision and calm hands. He's a surgeon, never drinks, likes to hunt for sport but always brings the meat home so in the basement freezer-chest there's antelope in a neat stack, venison in another stack, an icy globe of woodchuck in plastic and tin foil—a gift from Grandpa. Each white packet is labeled with the name of the animal, the date it was frozen.

My arm is tired, but I will not move. He puts on yellow shooting glasses, raises the gun to his neck, then stares at me for about ten seconds before he looks through the sight. We are parallel statues. I can feel the tall grass tickling my legs, the Buffalo grass under the pine trees bordering our lot, I keep my arm out, palm up fingers flat, the apple is perfect and shiny and O how much would I like to put it to my lips, to bite and taste it, to satisfy my desire for it.

And just as I begin to lose myself in the imaginary juicy chewing of the ripe sweet apple there is a loud crack and the orb grazes across my hand like a rope pulling through my fingers and then it's gone, shattered across the grass, yellow insides splayed about, a meal for birds. I look back. My dad lowers the gun. He pulls off his glasses and says *Good job.*

PART TWO

And nothing else; and nowhere
To go back to;
And no one else
As far as I know to verify.

—Charles Simic, *"A Wall"*

A TREE FOR YOU

Last summer, we drove to a tattoo
parlor, a day trip. I stood watching
a man named Ed shave your thigh;
you cringed as he placed the needle deep
near your tan line, carving a tree
without leaves, a bare tree you have wanted

for years now, ever since you wanted
to be free from your past. You thought a tattoo
on your hip would confess your freedom, like the tree
you'd climb to hide from your mother, watching
the back door, waiting for her to yell in her deep
yet polite voice, you resting the back of your thigh

on a high branch, amidst leaves. If she saw your thigh
now, you know what she'd say, if you wanted
to show her your blue tree, she'd look deep
into your blue eyes and remind you a tattoo
lasts forever. At Avon Kustom Tattoo, watching
with me were two burly men who saw the tree

grow, your skirt pulled up, black tree
ink staining the soft curve of your thigh,
my thumb in your clenched fist. You sweated, watching
to make sure the gloved hands made what you wanted
on your upper leg, a simple thin tattoo
of a tree, barren like one standing in the deep

of winter. Your mother was a deep,
complex woman, you once said; she knew the tree
was hiding you quietly, like how your new tattoo
hides under tights in winter, in summer your tan thigh
and the tree under loose skirts. You wanted
this since your college days in Vermont, watching

the huge old campus oaks like your mother watching
the tree, waiting for your skinny legs to drop from deep
within the lower leaves. She always wanted
a calm house for you, home should be safe, like your tree,
a form of solace like the tattoo on your thigh.
All these things are part of you. Your past is a tattoo;

your mother's watching eyes, the backyard tree,
they've left a deep mark on more than your thigh—
what you always wanted, a simple tattoo.

HOME, THE LAST TIME

There was always something to be fixed
at your mother's house—she gave you a list
each time you came home from college.
If you wavered, she would get angry,
do it herself—washing windows on a
beat-up ladder or smashing nails
into a loose chair leg. The leg still
rickety, nails twisted around
the wood spindle like a spider's legs.
You'd catch your socks on them, ripping holes—
more work for her, darning and sewing.

Every summer, there was the car to be
washed, the lawn that needed
mowing, the light fixtures to be cleaned,
littered with papery moths and cobwebs.
But when she's lying in a tall bed
on the 10th floor of the hospital,
in the quiet wing no one leaves alive,
the doctor tells you it's a matter
of weeks. He looks across his oak desk
and says you should clean out your emotions,
you need to say whatever it is
you have to say to her. You leave,
walk across the parking lot, imagine
a hand dusting and polishing your fear
of being called lazy or forgetful,
your resentment at the few times you
were unnoticed or undoted upon.

Every day in the pink hospice room
you wash her hands and face, then you feed her.
Today, there's chicken soup and crackers,
which she chews deliberately,
stopping every few seconds to rest.

When she's done, you push the tray away.
Before you're ready, she has
something to say, knows exactly what words
to use, but waits for the strength to speak.
As usual, she's gone ahead, not
willing to wait, while you lean passive
against the bed. Clear, rare elements
have collapsed her veins, bruised her hands and arms,
taken away her thick black hair,
but they haven't freed her body.
You wait until she's done, then you
hold out a tiny red milk carton
for her, let her reach for the straw,
lips pursed, eyes down, watching the white climb
toward her lips. In a week, you'll have
no more repairs to make, no floors to
sweep clean. Again, she's taken care of things.
Even her basement is cleared out,
leaving no trace of her, leaving you
with no chores to do, no light to make
brighter, no thing you can make
stand tall again.

CONTACT

Across from a line of houses, in an open
field of daisies and long grasses,
a spaceship landed, kicking up little dust.
Glinting saucer, spindly legged, B-movie
discard, but real. Cold and hard, steam hushing

from a vent underneath. All the neighborhood
came to see. They waited for a gangplank
to appear, for the bubble-eyed others to
shuffle down a black ramp
on frog-like paddlefeet and knees bent

backwards, or so they imagined.
The Kasinskis from down the street
brought lawn chairs. Fred from next door
came too, a can of beer in his hand,
hand resting on protruding belly. No one

said a word, words being careless and overused.
They waited, and waited some more.
To the west, someone painted the sky
red and pink, then purple. Nobody thought
to call the police. They merely watched,

shuffled their feet. Some teenage boys
edged closer in untied basketball shoes,
faces muddied by puberty;
red splotches, thin mustaches, odd big
noses and smartass smiles. One threw

a crabapple but missed the hull. Then one
sprinted under the ship, did a barrel run
around each stilt-leg. He stopped and banged
against the belly, open palm slapping.
Mother, Father, he yelled, his voice crackling

and high, *are you in there? Please, take me home.*
The others laughed and snorted, but the boy
kept knocking, kept asking. He wanted
to know low long he'd have to wait
before the world was going to end.

THE TRUTH ABOUT POETRY

Whatever it is,
it has no teeth,
will turn a smile
into a long wail
at any moment.
It cannot walk,
but aspires to.
It can't hold its head
without bobbing
and lolling
and will only taste
mother's word-milk,
its suckling mouth
yearning open,
on the cusp of drinking
a lifetime of syllables.

BROKE DOWN

The art of boozing isn't hard to master,
so I drink harder, drink faster,
drink to forget what I was meant to lose,
drop it into the trash can, can of refuse.

I'd like throw myself away awhile,
I'd like to go by dragging a birch tree
down toward the hard earth of frozen winter.
One should do more than merely be a drunk.

But on those blank, cold days, when I want to
feel fuzzy, when I want to be drunk,
there is nada for my eyes to see.
No glistening ice-streets, no faceless sky.

This cheap cotton-blend golf shirt I wear,
shrill shirt ballooning, how often it fails
to keep me warm, how it strains against my stooped
and uneven shoulders, just a thin sheet

of shivering. Fabric that's worthless and weak,
tin can soda man, lean green meadowlark,
my life is so stupid and difficult!
The IRS intending to levy,

the wife with legal representation and process servers,
my children—O!—who plain old don't like me.
The dog I had once, a happy furry puppy,
put down, put down,

the car I used to drive, in a junkyard
at the edge of town. Here I slouch on the couch,
can of beer on my gut. I'm a loser,
I'm a baby, can't think to drink

something sour-mashy and caustic—
et tu brutal stomach, not taking what I want
to give. I am the king of pain,
the one who does not seem, nay, but is,

the one who needs a shave and a couple new bits,
the one stuck with a mind of winter.

PACK MENTALITY

—For Tim Hale

You wake Sunday morning, it's 6:50, 10 minutes
'til you run. Your throat aches from beer, but practice
means at least 15 miles. You limp to the locker room,
don a shirt that won't chafe. Everyone's silent
until Coach comes down, handsome face all smiles,
and says, *Ellison Park.* You groan, not an easy

17 miler. The team begins with Westfall Road, easy
and flat, but you'll spend at least 50 minutes
loping the cracked asphalt; no sidewalks, just smiles
when you realize everyone's made it to practice,
even Dave, carrying a roll of TP in silence,
his face splotchy, Genesee beer-sweat making room

in his body for Gatorade. Your dorm-room
still has a girl in it, soft brown hair. She makes the run easier,
not thinking about tired-legs-cotton-mouth, but a silent
chant: *I got laid last night.* After thirty minutes
Coach's Chevette appears, following the practice—
he pulls up, sniffs at Dave and his cargo of TP, smiles,

Awww, Dave, what'sa matter? Stomach upset? Dave smiles
back weakly, you all laugh at his puffy eyes, no room
between him and the twelve of you. That's the way you practice,
bound tight in a leggy pack, it makes the miles easier.
Last night you drank together at frat houses, a few minutes
in each house. You have a bet going, who can piss in silence

against all the frat bars, pressed up by the masses, silently
opening your zippers, letting it flow, smiling
and holding out your plastic beer cup, a five-minute
wait before a dopey pledge fills yours. You leave those rooms
shouting *Death or Glory!* with your running mates, easily
your only soulmates, skinny guys with whom you practice

new levels of abuse. At this morning's practice
you reach the hills of Ellison Park and you're all silent,
one mind straining up the hill, hearing the easy
careless chirping birds. You fake a smile,
trying to love the pain. Later, in the training room,
you grab two bags of ice, lay on the grass for a few minutes

icing your shins in after-practice sun. You smile
when Dave lopes in silently and goes straight for the bathroom.
You feel easy, loose. There is bliss in these few minutes.

A FEVER OF POLLEN

You are like a honeybee seized in mindless
hovering, the sinewy wet between us

captures the moment like a held breath,
hipbones pressing in opposition. You climb

on fuzzy jointed legs, swabbed
in pollen, retracting and reaching,

honing in on nectar,
your sharp chitin face blushed

with the powdery makeup of wildflowers,
gauze wings fluttering a blur

as you slide over me, eyes dilated, slowly blinking.
You are light like a bone, your skin just

soft, your muscles tight as a cord
along your spine, breathing along

my fingers as I take you into
my lungs, exchange dust and air

for your sacred skin and brushing hair.
And then, you wane. Rise over

this saccharine passive flower
on spindly limbs, hover

then lift, a spinning
airy motor, then fall

away, our separate
skin cooling and dry.

WHEN IT DISOBEYS

it brings a storm that discovers
a man-made river bed in concrete
and asphalt, leaves women and men
clinging to rooftop chimneys,
their cold hands trembling in its midst, then
it brings the hail—white, killing,
obnoxious white when there
should be more rain—first pea
then quarter then softball
sized, full of hubris,
stony pellets coursing
through streets, a swirling
river of rain and downed trees and things
dismantled. Will it not
avoid stinging the innocent faces,
the defeated shoulders—
will it not give up the mindless idea
that it can last in August?
It is relentless, abiding by precepts
which are not laws
but ideas of laws, things
children copy down in school:
Planets in their ellipses,
the moon's granite face
waning and waxing,
cosmic dust on a calm night—
meteors burning their light,
known for a second, then gone,
like the faraway shouts
and moans when the sky
clears and a rainbow comes.

COMPLICATIONS

The moment one begins to speak,
complications set in. English
is the bastard child of thought,
thought is a mother who's impetuous

and odd. She wears bright lipstick
looking less than classy, she wraps
her hair in cheap nylon scarves
and will not look you in the eye.

Careless, she does not consider
this child—English–or any
of her squealing, mutating babies.
They've been left on the brick doorstep

of mouths, left to fend for themselves
in tattered clothes and bare feet,
runny noses and productive coughs.
They beg the ear for help, for utterance,

but those swirling appendages
attached to heads in tophats, to necks
in mink coats and swishing taffeta,
merely use these children, like crude tools,

to seize what they lust after.
If silence is satisfaction, then desire
is a sentence—an action performed
with some goal demarcated,

something grand like eternal love,
or small, like a sunflower seed.
What else would make the parrot
speak through his callous beak?

HORSES

Always, the learning begins with words.
First are simple expressions, to be recited
by a child. Back, tail, ear,

hoof, nose. Then, others
full of nuance and suggestive intent—
mane, canon bones, bridge, wither.

Once you learn the body you come to know
the gear, its rich aroma
of oil and leather, chocolate

or deep black with gleaming rivets.
There is the lead rope, the shanks,
the bridle joined to the bit,

the ready saddle. And after
the mount there are more: words
that move the rippling legs—

walk, trot, yield, and finally,
stand, when the animal rests,
attentive to the shrug of your thighs,

the angle of your hips.
Canter and gallop come next,
meant to convey speed,

the way the forest around a
trail degenerates into a green blur,
the almost concurrent pound of three

hooves, then a pause as the mount
gathers, collects her legs, and spurs
forth with muscled power.

Only then can you fully speak the fluid
elegance of these animals, their dark eyes,
personae as distinct and sharp

as their smell—Appaloosa,
Saddlebred, Thoroughbred, Arabian,
Royal Lippizon, Warmblood.

Only then will you know that horses
are beautiful for themselves, but also for
their conjuring, their spell of words.

A BARGAIN FOR JOE

Joe wept when he listened to
calypso music on his Walkman,
bronzing himself on a shell-strewn beach
in a true self-gloat. Consumed
by nostalgia, he bargained with gods,
turned away from a chance
to live in sun and sand forever. "Take me back
to my ranch house on Willow Lane," he begged,
"back to my pickup with the rusted bed,
my beer-can collection, my dog-eared
Mickey Spillane paperbacks."
The gods looked favorably on his want,
his desire for Fenway Franks, warm Budweiser,
and Joe endured the barter well,
agreeing to make a pilgrimage on foot,
hoofing it all the way to a land-locked
shopping plaza where he'd slam
a giant oar, bizarre tower of tithing,
into the hot, parking lot asphalt.
Just to mock the perfect, white
beach which now whispers calypso
music: sweet, clanging, percussive.

DEIDRE PLAYS BASS FOR ME

Deidre, my neighbor and sometime lover, looks serious
when she plays bass guitar—but then her eyes

always look that way; clouded and dark, a diabetic gaze.
Scars on her shins, pink and tight,

remind her a scratch takes months to heal,
a slow, artless wound. She keeps saying she wants to be

cremated, she fears blindness more
than losing her legs, though she doesn't check her blood,

will not pierce her fingertip, draw out a small sphere
of red. She tells me her life is half over at 27;

the rest is decline and the loss of toes. This is the life
she's supposed to lead, she says. We all have to die

of something, and she knows what that something is.
But then she tells me she's quit smoking again,

nine days clean, no more chemical need, only
the mental battle now. Behind me on the wall

hangs her ideal lover—an Elvis poster, all slick hair
and sly smile, cheeks covered with lipstick kisses.

To my left, in the unused fireplace, three ceramic flamingos—
pink arching necks, pencil legs. On the coffee table,

next to her glass of Absolut and cranberry juice,
lies a scattered pile of clear syringes in orange caps.

They tremble as music vibrates from her strings and she plays
a halting lullaby, "Jane Says," low and high notes

rolling over one another like a pair of lazy cats.
Deidre plays bass for me, her captive.

ELVIS IDEAL

Photograph

He's on the floor, everyone gawking as if he's
tripped or fainted, anguish in everyone's hips,
in their lips, slightly open, mouths deep

black circles. Camera bulbs are about to
flash, all the women are standing, hands by
their faces probably trembling or held up

to praise Jesus for letting them see
Him, see the soles of his shoes, the way
his head dips from his shoulders, caressing

the microphone with sweet, puckered lips.
Everyone in the theatre leans toward him like
shavings of steel

toward a magnet. Does he think of them
as he crawls across the dusty stage, hard wood
pain in his elbows and knees? Does he hear

them, or is he one with the music,
unaware of the storm he makes, those pulled
crazy by the voice singing through his body?

Records

Driving cross country, I stop at Graceland,
my car the color of dust from many states.
It is a mansion cliché: the jungle room,
the white room, the burgundy billiard room.

The grounds have a presence that is absence, the silence
of a room after a lover has left. I wander with the tour group
to the racquetball court, now a wall of gold and platinum
records, the locker-room filled with cases of Elvis perfume,

Elvis sneakers, Elvis pencil erasers. On wire figures, his polyester
Phoenix outfit, his comeback special black leather jumper,
two pairs of thick gold sunglasses. A guide tells us
the pantsuits gave him "ease of movement."

Outside, a blind vacuum twists through the water.
We step up to the gravestones. I know he's not really there.
Out in the meadow near the bustling road,
I see his Palomino, a sturdy old horse, munching bluegrass.

Time

I have an Elvis wall clock, numbers
on his chest and chin, hands open
at his sides, mouth open
in mid-song, legs and hips swinging—
a pendulum keeping time.

Together

January 8th. My wife and I tune in to Elvis 101, a station
playing The King all day. We listen to "In the Ghetto"
and she laughs. We listen to "Suspicious
Minds" and I am sad, too sad.

All day it goes like this.
We only speak when it's important, to make a flip
comment or tell a story about something.
It grows dark. The day has slid by.

When they play "All Shook Up" a fifth time, we turn the radio off.
I sit on the couch, looking at the faces of the tall buildings
outside our downtown loft, their endless cubes of light.
I pray someone is in there, dusting.

PART THREE

Tell me as you labour hard
To break this unrelenting soil,
What barns are there for you to fill?
What farmer dragged you from the boneyard?

—Seamus Heaney, *"The Digging Skeleton"*

THRUWAY MALL ATRIUM, 1980

I shuffle my brown clogs against the
Astroturf risers as Mr. Vogel mouths out
the title of our next song, "In the Mood."
It is February, the mall is scattered
with old couples and a few parents;
the Cleveland Hill High School Stage Band
entertains shoppers, an afternoon of jazz and swing.
I'm second chair trombone even though
I sometimes fake playing when the notes
come too fast, throwing the slide back and forth—
I think I look good without sounding bad.
But "In the Mood" is easy, and I shift
my arm smoothly, a confident 14-year-old,
pulling and pushing the slide, lips pressed
against the silver mouthpiece. The band's in sync,
and Mr. Vogel allows himself a smile
for the small crowd near a stand of plastic ferns.
Ron Lyon's parents are there—
he's first trombone, has a sound
I'll never create, a rich, silky aura that flows
from his gleaming Cohn trombone.
And then, by the penny-filled water fountain
I see my father, in his post office uniform;
in the light of the plexiglas atrium
I notice his sandy-blonde mustache,
something I've taken for granted,
he's had it so long. He waves shyly,
adjusting his empty mailbag. His eyes
don't seem tired in this light, though
he's been sleeping on the couch since August.
I've never seen his face while I play—
I practice in the basement
so he can hear Dan Rather.
Yet there he is, my only witness.

By next September, I'll outgrow
these brown clogs and quit
Mr. Vogel's stage band. Before that,
my father will move to an apartment
three blocks from the mall. He'll sleep alone
in a small room, he'll eat off paper plates.
During Ron's solo, a smooth melodic swing,
I count out the measures and smile at my father,
whose face, different now, smiles back.

ON SAFARI

When I am eaten by a lean,
proud lioness I will grow
minuscule and spend my days
lounging in her sloshy stomach,
I will shadowbox in the light
from her eardrums,
speed punching her epiglottis,
making her cough.
In the morning, I will wake
and clean between
her teeth with my shoelaces,
I will scrape her tongue for
bacteria, I will make her
sneeze awake
by hopping
through the slick
caverns of her nose.
She will be empty inside,
with living space
galore, her ribs a jungle gym
for me to climb on.
I will tickle the nerves
along her spine on the small
of her back and her legs
will grow weak and she will sit
and one leg will absently
scratch at air.
In the outside world,
all my appointments
will be canceled, my job given
to an underling,
my house foreclosed and sold
at auction.

I will thrive in the belly
and body of my
love, my lioness.
I will smell the sweet savanna
grasses of Africa when she breathes.
I will develop a taste
for raw meat and the chase.

LIGHT

—For AED

I sometimes picture myself a small boy
looking out a vast glass window, waiting.

I want to tell him you will be
coming soon, he will be yours

when you find him, years away.
I want to see this boy turn from the window,

open the door to find you—bright girl
with golden hair and azure eyes—

on his doorstep. Please tell him
to be safe, the way you tell me now,

when I'm driving into the mountains,
into the dull light of falling snow.

Tell him to be careful, to be happy,
for you will soon be in his life, you will light

it for him, making the world more vivid
than he's ever seen. All he must do is wait.

HALLOWEEN SATELLITE

Tall trees shake as the wind blows cold.
Miniature gangs clamber along sidewalks,
onto porches and down again,
complex pattern and grid. Our daughter skips,

glistening silver in the dusk light,
dying earth lamp. Her small form is a stellar
case, but really just a cardboard box in tin foil
with solar panels arching out, like wings.

On her head, a bike helmet, also in foil,
antennae bobbing. She is a silver butterfly,
but really she is a satellite. Her orbit
is not an ellipse but a zig-zag toward

neighbors with bowls of bright sugar,
doling out handfuls to the throngs
of hoboes, ballerinas, vampires. She careens
past them, their chatter cosmic static.

Soon, when the sky grades down to night
and the hum of streetlamps, she will, like Sputnik,
like SkyLab, come down to earth, into our cold hands.
But while she sings through the thin gray of late day

she is like us, carrying a message across vast fields
of electric air, like me, now, using crude tools to
carry a message to those in the ether,
in the dark earth, ashes and dust.

AT THE WATER

My mother's dry cough echoes down the hall,
her feet creaking the floorboards. It's an old house, wallpaper of
dull blue and yellow flowers, horse-hair plaster bowed out and
cracked, failing under its own weight.

Weight. I see her down the hallway, glimpse of nightgown.

The gown's cloth sighs as she pivots into
her room. The hall is empty, sun streams through
a window by the stairs, burning white curtains.
She groans, sits on the bed, leans into pillows.

And blankets. The headboard bangs softly, then nothing.

Nothing. Mid-afternoon. She has tried to
inhabit her weariness, a black cloak.
Most days are like this. Most days, she walks out
of the last room; most days she goes back.

Back. At Singing Beach. The rim of water,

still water, the surface a mirror that reflects
a silver-gray sky. Barefoot, she digs her toes
into the cold. She lifts her arms, pulls off
her nightgown. Her skin is white, pure, and unscarred.

Pure. She steps into the water, stops

at her thighs. Dips her hands in, from her hands
she drinks. Silver drops from cupped palms.
She kneels, thick trunk of her back, spine mounded.
Slowly. She slips down, until nothing is left.

Nothing is left but a circular wake where she has gone under.

DOLPHINETTES

—For Michelle and Susan

In the cavernous pool stadium,
music flourishes as I slide onto a bench.
A spotlight cuts the darkness,
a white halo circles
my sisters on the deck.
When their golden bodies
slip into the water, giving forth
shards of brittle light,

the audience is dazzled in the dark.
Two young women, as much me
as anything, dance as one geisha
with four dark eyes, four elegant hands weaving
to the music, twenty toes pointed,
feet arched into little crescent-moons,
gliding in unity as if
fishing line binds them together—

wrist to wrist, elbow to elbow,
hips and ankles—as if shared blood
has coordinated every sinew.
They float, supple backs pressed into the surface.
They smile at us and duck under,
to another world I dream of still:
sky blue tile, navy lane markers,
the deep end a quarry of placid

weightlessness. I don't know how they hold
their breath so long, their nostrils crimped closed
by noseplugs. They've merely gone under,
transfigured into tendrils of color,
skin and suit, the spotlight staying
with them until two left legs appear,

gleaming and taut, each like a
dolphin's tail, twirling in perfect time.

A half turn, then another, then another.
In dreams, I see those toes become
webbed, a thin veneer of scale emerges,
then noseplugs drift down, gills opening
under each rib, eyelids shedding,
my sisters perfecting a dance
as fish, leaving me in the loud, dry world
for the blue, the blue I still dream.

NED FALLS

Trapped at swim team practice, I stand under fluorescent lights.
My fingers are wrinkled carrots waiting to be peeled, my toes are
webbed, the water is cold and greenish,

the natatorium air is musty and chlorinated, my eyes want to
be rubbed as Ned dives in with a loud splash but no spray.
I hear his body warp under waves.

Ned's our star, my fingers are pencils pointing out his taut shoulders,
my shoulders are rounded like the glass paperweight Mr. Kowalski,
our Algebra teacher, keeps on his desk. Inside, a frozen scorpion

curls to strike. Ned can faint on command, spilling his
books across the floor. His body splayed out, eyes vacant, tongue
rolling between his lips like an overheated dog.

After practice, the open sky will drown out all except the cawing
blackbirds who school in trees. Ned will climb the top branches,
conversing with them, his skin growing feathers, his fingers
    scraping talons.

When the season begins Ned will swim fast as a manta ray,
he'll be a terse racer, water will bloom over the guttered sides
onto the deck, sticky with the growth of mossy germs.

Ned believes in *mens sana in corpore sana*.
Yesterday, the diving board tripped Ned, throwing him in.
He looked dead under the ripples, but I knew he was just holding
    his breath.

ALBANY WINTER

After John Cheever's "The Swimmer"

In the foyer closet by the staircase
he finds a silk scarf, smells the lingering
sweetness, tangerine and cream,
his dry fingertips snagging the
soft weave. He ponders the call
of a bullfrog by the backyard pool,
cannot believe it's gone, all of it,
nothing left except dust on windowsills,
a lonely, white scarf.
He blames himself—he coveted
too much for it to be good. She is far away,
the kids dispersed to distant gray cities,
the house—incredibly—empty,
and he can see a time, years from now,
when he'll be old and so in love
with this moment that he'll have to
get up from the table and make tea,
whiskey or vodka too harsh. He'll sip
hot sweetness from an old mug, listen
to his grandfather's cabin creak
on a raw cold night. Only then
will he love this moment, when he is old
and alone and lonely: the scarf against
his face, bitterness on his tongue, the taste
of emptiness. The wind will stamp outside,
night falling in a small window,
winter, the fields golden and dead,
just outside Albany, in the old house
with gravestones down back by the creek
in the shadow of a dormant willow,
his family name eroded,
but the strange skulls and wings
of death still clear, still indelible.

OCTOBER TRAVELS, WIND RIVER RANGE

—For Bill Henderson

Last night, in our nylon tents,
we were tempted by the wolves again,
their howls curling around

our camp. This morning I knew
our trip was over.
We slouched along the valley

toward our cars, in our heads
some eternal progress we'd amassed
in the cold nights. We were like ravens,

picking at traces in the dust and leaves,
a different language left behind, straggling
forms in a fog, now barely on the ridge.

We learned this and walked.
The wolves were silent.
Then to the west, a thin slot

appeared, a pale blue swath, then gold light
illuminating, our bodies walking
away from the wolves.

WHISPER, IN A DARK SUIT

I go back only to bury the dead. The flights
are pricey and dreamless. The weather is ice

cold, brutally so. Then, the funeral home: soft lights,
gleaming bronze, my hands in pockets.

I whisper, in a dark suit. Then I stand above
a hole in the earth, on dormant

bluegrass fed by Mother's decay,
Grandfather's no-more flesh. I take it

like a man, then fly home. I lie awake
in the night-room, remember the before.

THE FAR BADLANDS

In that solitude of soundless things, in the random
company of the wind, to be weightless, nameless.—Mark Strand

Here, the wind has no trees to make it sing—
it hushes onward, a low hovering sigh.
Hiking from the dirt road, I avoid trails and campsites,
my steps sinking into dry earth,
sometimes sliding crab-like down steep faces

on heels and hands, tearing off a skin
of crumbled dirt. An hour of
travel and there is no one.
This is what I came for, to be alone,
my face unseen, voice silent.

In the midst of the Badlands
there is nothing to hear but the wind
gliding past like a snake.
On a distant plateau, buffalo
stand still, become statues.

Watching them, my walking
becomes an enigma,
I'm nothing but footsteps in a crooked line,
soon to be washed away by the careless
grind of wind and rainwater.

When dusk comes, I set up camp,
sit cross-legged as the sun
blazes the western rim of sky.
Every second the clouds' purple
deepens, chameleons of sunset.

In this open space, I know
the day's failing glow, the sweep
of my watch's second hand.
In this open air, stars pierce through
to form mythic heroes and creatures

as the Badlands fade away,
and then I sleep.
Before dawn, I strike camp. The wind
rests. I walk slow, unable to sense
direction, walled in by a swirling maze

of dry stream beds and spires of rock
capped by tufts of sagebrush.
I come up and over a small hill: a herd of mule deer
freeze, all eyes on me. Another step
and they bound away, white tails raised.

When I reach the overlook parking lot
and open the car door, there's my face,
dimly in the window. Seconds later,
the sun breaks the horizon and warms the world.
In Cedar Pass, just outside the gates of the Park,

an old Sioux in a faded jean jacket
slouches in a folding chair,
gray hair cascading
over his shoulders. He too
looks for my face as I pump the gas.

ODE TO THE PACIFIERS

Let those scorn you who never
Starved in your dearth —Robert Pinsky

Comfort elixir, sleep-dozer, quiet-plug,
O how you have saved me,
O how you have buttoned and plugged
those grumpy weary O mouths,
O how you have waved sadnesses
away and made darkness a time for dreams.
Mam, Nuk, The First Years—3317,
molded in Austria, Germany, Taiwan, Philippines,
you are the juicy bait from which I catch
my babyfishes, pull them out of their ocean
of cry and fuss, gently drop them
into the hold in the hull of our house,
where they drift, the new cells
which I have half-made.
Your swallow-guard, hip cradles
under nose, your end a knob
that turns off the volume,
sometimes with a handle
like a purse-strap, your business end
a tan flexible light bulb, fake nipple,
idea bubble, bald man's mini-head, dirigible,
future tooth crookener they sometimes say—
but really? I do love you so,
I have worshipped you, genuflected to you
even though you weave dust and fibers
and momma-hair around
your saliva-slick end,
even though you always disappear,
falling and scattering like a mouse
under counters, car tires, beds,
into heating vents, garbage disposals,
et cetera, et cetera.

Though I have never French-kissed
you clean, I will never accuse you
of badness. But I do
worry, some nights when I can't sleep,
nights they are with you: who will someday
coddle them, what will they suckle
if they end up on dark streets
with cruisers, sharks, and other bad
men, my girls gazing into locked storefronts,
their shoelaces untied,
fingernails dirty and uncut, their bodies—
skin and bone that I have so
carefully wrought—grimy and cold?

BLUE HAZE, GOODNIGHT MOON

Black smoke courses along the blank hills,
there is a crack that runs the length of it.

Shouts in far-off dusk, I park. The engine ticks.
Early night heat, late September. Soon the leaves

will collapse their canopies, like so many
umbrellas. Then the summer of fire

will no longer burn my lungs
or clot my eyes, those plumes

stretching from the west.
Upstairs, the kids are asleep, white noise

the shape of a running fan, night light burning
their room gold from within,

a glistening cocoon.
Ten o'clock. I tip-toe in, listen to their sleep,

gaze at their shadow features.
It is like drinking cold water from a well.

CPSIA information can be obtained
at www.ICGtesting.com
Printed in the USA
FSOW01n1314250517
34666FS